Power Down for Fitness
Yoga for Flexible Mind and Body

Marko Galjasevic and Deborah Wood

RED CHAIR
·PRESS·

Let's Move books are produced and published by Red Chair Press.

Red Chair Press LLC   PO Box 333   South Egremont, MA 01258

www.redchairpress.com

Note

Look for notes through out this book directed to adults and caregivers.
Notes provide background and guidance for each exercise and movement.

Publisher's Cataloging-In-Publication Data

Names: Galjasevic, Marko. | Wood, Deborah, 1977-

Title: Power down for fitness: yoga for flexible mind and body / Marko Galjasevic and Deborah Wood.

Description: South Egremont, MA : Red Chair Press, [2018] | Series: Let's move | Includes index, glossary, and suggestions for further reading. | Interest age level: 006-010. | Summary: "Kids know exercise is good for them. But they may not know there are different kinds of exercise ... This book presents easy-to-follow yoga poses for kids plus informational notes for adults who dare to join them in stretching for flexibility and fitness."--Provided by publisher.

Identifiers: ISBN 9781634404105 (library hardcover) | ISBN 9781634404129 (paperback) | ISBN 9781634404143 (ebook)

Subjects: LCSH: Yoga--Juvenile literature. | Physical fitness for children--Juvenile literature. | CYAC: Yoga. | Physical fitness.

Classification: LCC RA781.7 .G35 2018 (print) | LCC RA781.7 (ebook) | DDC 613.7/046083/4$a[E]--dc23

LCCN: 2017957079

Illustrations: BPI India Pvt. Ltd.

Photographs: iStock

Printed in the United States of America

0518 1P CGBF18

Table of Contents

Types of Exercise. 4

What Is Yoga?. 5

Introduction 6

The Poses (Asanas)

Balloon Belly 8

Egg Pose/Child's Pose. 10

Mountain/Tree Pose 12

Down-Dog/Upward Dog 14

Cobra Pose 16

Warrior Pose 18

Moon Pose 20

Crow Pose 22

Basket Pose. 24

Butterfly Pose 26

Bee's Breath 28

Resting Pose 29

Words to Know 30

Read More 31

Index/About the Authors. 32

TYPES OF EXERCISE

You know exercise is good for you. But you might not know that there are different kinds of exercise. Each helps your body in different ways.

The great news is that a lot of what you like to do probably counts as at least one of these types of exercise. And maybe even more than one. For example, running works your heart and lungs, your muscles, and makes your bones strong.

Different kinds of exercise are:

1. **Aerobic exercise** to get your heart pumping,

2. **Muscle-strengthening exercise** to make you strong,

3. **Stretching exercise** to make your muscles bend and move easily. Toe touches and side bends are good for **flexibility**. But let's learn about a science that is thousands of years old to help stretch our bodies. It is called **yoga**!

What is Yoga?

Yoga is a science that is very old. It is a science of the mind and body. A pose, or the way the body moves in yoga is called **asana**. You do the poses by moving your body into different shapes. But yoga is also about calming your mind. The asanas shown in this book help to stretch the body, build strength, and give you energy. The practice may even help you sleep better.

Introduction

How should you use this book? Focus on having fun with the poses, not on doing each one perfectly. Notice how moving the body can change the way you feel and how you breathe. Try using some of these poses throughout the day. (Although poses that are back bending, like "basket pose," give you energy, so you might want to avoid these before bedtime!) Be patient and keep trying. And most importantly have fun together as a family!

The practice of yoga integrates the mind and body by using the breath, you could think of it as the tether between the two. It is what helps us to be present in the moment and quiet the chatter of the mind. Even a very simple yoga practice can free us from stress and anxiety—it works for kids and adults! Simple tools like feeling your feet on the ground, locating yourself in the space you are in, and slowing down the breath can help children to find shelter in their own bodies, self-soothe, and act receptively instead of being reactive. Not only do the poses stretch, strengthen, and energize the body, which is good for physical health, but the poses can help manage sensory or emotionally overwhelming experiences. How? These mind-body practices stimulate the parasympathetic nervous system (rest-and-digest). This restorative system of the body decreases blood pressure, the heart rate, and stress hormone production.

Developing mind-body awareness through yoga empowers kids with their own inner-strength. It cultivates communication and a respect for the body, improves focus and attention, sleep, and decreases stress and anxiety. The poses in this book are easy to learn and fun to practice. Children will be able to store them away in their toolbox for life. Poses like "upward facing dog" energize the body and combat prolonged sitting, while forward folding poses like "egg pose" are calming.

"Mountain pose" improves posture and concentration. "Warrior pose" trains the mind to feel the body while building confidence. Simply learning to breathe well helps to manage stress. You see, all of these poses serve a greater purpose.

Balloon Belly
Adham Pranayama

Sit with your legs crossed and place your hands on your belly. Slowly breathe in through your nose and fill your belly like a balloon.

Note

When anxiety strikes, our sympathetic nervous system is activated to fight, flee, or freeze. Focusing on deep diaphragmatic breathing can help soothe the system back to a calm state. This works for both kids and adults!

Keeping your mouth closed, slowly breathe out and
empty the balloon. Notice your hand moving up
and down with your belly balloon. Fill your balloon
five to ten times.

Egg Pose
Balasana

Sit back on your heels and bring your forehead to the ground. Curl yourself up into a tiny ball just like an egg! Take five slow, deep breaths through your nose. Place your arms loosely on the floor by your sides.

Note

Not only does this pose stretch the back and shoulders, but it can be a comforting tool for self-care. Anyone can take shelter in this easy pose. This pose is often called the Child's Pose.

Now, stretch your arms in front of you with your fingertips on the ground. How does this make you feel?

Mountain Pose
Tadasana

Stand with your feet together and your shoulders rolled back. Imagine you are as tall and strong as a mountain. Mountains don't move. Can you be as still as a mountain? Now slowly lift your arms over your head. Stand taller!

Note

This pose brings stillness and calm to the mind. The balance found in the external body becomes internal balance. This pose also builds self-confidence in children. Stand tall!

Tree Pose
Vriksasana

Stand on your right foot. Bring your left foot to the inside of your right thigh or ankle. Reach your hands up to the sky. You're a tree! Trees can balance like this for hundreds of years. Can you try to balance for five seconds? Now, try it on the other side.

On which side was it easier to balance?

Note

Grounding and rooting through the feet helps to reestablish presence in the body, and reduces anxious thoughts. This pose builds confidence and focus.

Down-Facing Dog and Up-Facing Dog

Adho Mukha Svanasana and Urdhva Mukha Svanasana

Stand on your hands and feet. Press them down into the ground and lift your hips up high to the sky. Drop your head down, just like a dog sniffing the ground. Shake your tail!

Note

These poses stretch and strengthen the entire body. Doing this a few times is a great way for kids to move energy through the body before they need to sit still and focus. Next time, try it before sitting down to do homework!

Now drop your hips to the ground and look up. Howl like a dog howling at the moon!

Can you do this three times? Do you have more energy?

Cobra Pose
Bhujangasana

Lay on your belly. Press your hands into the ground and lift your chest up while keeping your legs and hips on the ground. Hiss like a snake!

Note

This pose stretches the shoulder, chest, and belly, along with removing stiffness in the lower back. Backbends decrease fatigue, and bring fresh energy to body and mind—the perfect antidote to sitting in a car or at a desk!

Warrior Pose
Virabhadrasana

Stand with your legs wide apart. Turn the right foot out and bend your leg. Extend your arms out long and wide like arrows.

Note

This powerful pose stretches the hips and shoulders, opens the lungs, and energizes the entire body. It helps to develop balance, stability, and confidence.

Hold this pose for three to five breaths, and say, "I AM STRONG!"

Don't forget to do this on the other side!

Moon Pose
Ardha Chandrasana

Stand tall! Bend forward and place your right hand on the ground in front of your right foot. Lift your left leg up to the sky. Can you lift your left arm up to your side? Try it! Imagine you are floating in the sky like the moon.

Note

This is another pose that brings attention to the present moment through focusing on balance. Balancing poses help to shift the focus out of our heads and bring it back into our bodies, which has a stabilizing effect. It is also a great pose to practice falling! Laugh, and then get up and try again!

Practice your "moon pose" on the other side. Can you hold it and count to ten?

Crow Pose
Bakasana

Squat like a frog. Then, place your hands on the floor. Tuck your knees into your armpits. Now lift your feet up and take flight like a crow! If you can't lift both feet up at once, then try one foot at a time.

Note

This pose is fun. It allows kids to fall safely and try, try again. Crow pose develops upper body strength and focus. It cultivates coordination and confidence.

If you feel like you're falling, tuck your head and do a somersault!

Basket Pose
Dhanurasana

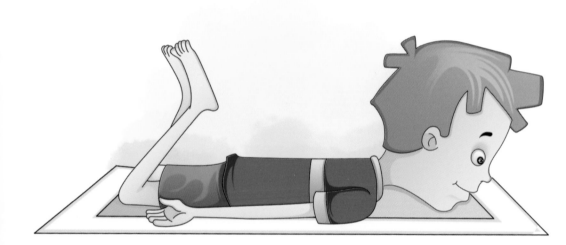

Lay flat on your belly with your arms along the sides of your body. Bend your knees, reach your arms back, and grab your ankles or shins. Breath in and reach your heels up towards the sky.

Note

Often called the Bow Pose, this is another fatigue buster! It tones the arms and legs, adds greater flexibility to the spine, and opens up the chest which allows for a deeper breath to calm the nervous system. And, it's fun to do!

Lift your heart up! Lift your thighs off of the floor!
You've shaped your body into a basket! Try to rock
back and forth without letting go of your ankles.

Butterfly Pose
Baddha Konasana

Sit down on the ground. Bend your knees and bring the bottoms of your feet together.

Note

This forward fold is another tool your child can use to self-soothe and reset. Breathing slow and deep while in this pose can also help manage stress or feelings of being overwhelmed.

Sit tall and flap your knees up and down like a butterfly! You may want to slowly fold over your legs like a sleeping butterfly. Let your head hang heavy. What color are your wings?

Bee's Breath
Bhramari Pranayama

Sit with your legs crossed. Close your eyes and ears. Take a deep breath in. Exhale with your mouth closed and make a humming sound like a bee. How long can you buzz like a bee with one breath? Buzz five to seven times before you breathe in again.

Note

This breathing exercise can help to release frustration, stress, and anger. On the inhale you could ask your child to think of what is bothering them, scoop it up, and on the exhale (buzzing) let it go. It really works!

Resting Pose
Savasana

Find a position where you can be very still, quiet, and calm. Maybe it is lying on your back with your palms facing up to the sky. Maybe you can find this stillness lying on your side with your knees bent.

Once you find your resting spot wiggle your arms and your legs. Wiggle your whole body one final time! Then be still like a sleeping bug. If you are comfortable, close your eyes. Let every part of your body feel heavy and sink into the ground. Practice resting.

Note

This resting pose helps the body and mind to assimilate the benefits of yoga. It allows your child (and you!) to process the practice and settle deeply. If you can, dim the lights and make the room very quiet. All of the other poses led up to this very important pose! Remember your child can practice resting like this any time of day. Five to ten minutes is all it takes to restore and reset.

WORDS TO KNOW

asana: a yoga posture

diaphragmatic breathing: deep breathing done by contracting the abdomen and expanding the belly

flexibility: to bend easily and without breaking.

parasympathetic nervous system: a part of the nervous system responsible for "rest and digest" in the body; helps produce equilibrium.

pranayama: breathing exercises; breath control

sympathetic nervous system: a part of the nervous system responsible for "fight or flight" in the body; prepares our body for action in response to stress.

yoga: a mind-body science that's thousands of years old; a practice of postures and breathing to keep the body healthy and calm the mind.

READ MORE

Books for Kids

Engel, Christiane. *ABC Yoga*. Walter Foster, Quarto Publishing Group, 2016.

Lebrecque, Ellen. *Flexibility: Stretch and Move Further!* Heinemann-Raintree, 2013.

Taeeun Yoo. *You Are a Lion: and other Fun Yoga Poses*. Nancy Paulsen Books, Penguin, 2012.

Verde, Susan. *I Am Yoga*. Abrams, 2015.

Books for Adults

Harper, Jennifer Cohen. *Little Flower Yoga for Kids: A Yoga and Mindfulness Program to Help Your Child Improve Attention and Emotional Balance*. New Harbinger Publications, 2013.

Snel, Eline. *Sitting Still Like a Frog: Mindfulness Exercises for Kids* (and their Parents). Shambhala, 2013.

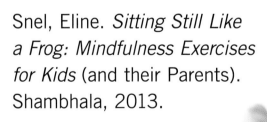

INDEX

Balloon Belly 8

Basket Pose 24

Bee's Breath............28

Butterfly Pose 26

Cobra Pose 16

Crow Pose...............22

Down Dog..............14

Egg Pose 10

Moon Pose..............20

Mountain Pose 12

Resting Pose 29

Tree Pose 13

Warrior Pose............18

About the Authors

Deborah Wood and **Marko Galjasevic** have over a decade of experience bringing yoga and wellness to students of all ages. Originally from New York City, they teach yoga in upstate New York where they live with their daughter.